Acid Virga

Gabriel Kruis

PRAISE FOR *ACID VIRGA*

"In the Southwest we have personal agonies that are nothing in the face of that landscape. Then, we go to New York and give the self up to being a beautiful style, the New York School (I have done this), remaining haunted. Gabriel Kruis is a really formidable poet. *Acid Virga*, is rather terrifying, also a tour de force and a formal breakthrough... a blend of narrative and lyric the way the mind is, mixing New Mexico and New York the way the mind does because it's one mind, or the mind of one body. If you get very fast (using Jimmy Schuyler's short line that after all is kind of slow) you can dissolve all the mental barriers we've been taught to erect between kinds of experiences. 'I don't know where I am, what / story I'm telling anymore—'"
—Alice Notley

"As wildly visionary as it is linguistically alive, Gabriel Kruis's *Acid Virga,* drills down into the bedrock of American life to produce a book unparalleled in its exploration of how visionary experience and social upheaval collide in ways that are both transformative and annihilating. Like Blake, Kruis 'has set his forehead against the ignorant Hirelings' in this series of extended meditations on social decay and religion, erotic life and drug and drug addiction, the life of the spirit and the letter of the law, and the subconscious ways in which relations between parent and child become ghost structures that make and maim us in later life. His disabused yearnings for the sublime are tempered by a fiercely analytical intelligence that allows for maximum fluidity of conception achieved with maximum hardness of execution."
—Tom Sleigh

"Reading Gabriel Kruis's *Acid Virga* had a profound and lasting effect on me. I marvelled in his language and formal innovations which are rich with familiar references yet surprising at the same time. Many great poets know how to do these things. What makes this work singular is the more difficult to articulate sense that each word on the page has a double that is working on us... at a cellular level, creating space to connect the particulars of one's life story with the historical. Words serve as flowers with 'pastel codes of grief.' Or bones the earth wants to cough up. If you've ever been conscious, and felt a little disturbed about it, of life as ancient and ephemeral or that falling apart is an integral force, this is a book to read over and over."

—Stacy Szymaszek

"As with most gorgeous and stolid debuts, a great affliction and affection inform *Acid Virga*, fast-moving with strophes like brisk moving cloud banks over the mind in your heart. Gabriel Kruis takes us further passionately into memory, grief, and wonder, as he hovers in language where 'volt by volt / of synapses fluttering' could mean we have arrived at thresholds of understanding or another kind of hunger. In either case, what a voice to enter our lives at this moment, full of terror and joy, like a young Miguel Hernandez."

—Major Jackson

Published in the United States by:
Archway Editions, a division of powerHouse Cultural Entertainment, Inc.
32 Adams Street
Brooklyn, NY 11201
e-mail: info@powerHouseBooks.com
website: www.archwayeditions.us

Library of Congress Control Number: 2020946375

ISBN 978-1-57687-970-2

Printed by Friesens Corp.

First edition, 2020

10 9 8 7 6 5 4 3 2 1

Printed and bound in Canada

Design intern: Emily Bluedorn
Interior layout by Robert Avellan
Book design by Francesca Richer

Cover Image: *Golden Showers* by Nicole Eisenman (2000)

EDITIONS

Acid Virga

Gabriel Kruis

Archway Editions, Brooklyn, NY

For E, in whom I've found a home

CONTENTS

SAY

"Poetry's air,
Money's ore," Or,
"Poetry's a kind-of
money,"

Say,
"Dirt & not copper makes a color darker,
It makes the shape
so heavy
& makes no melody
harder,"

Or,
"Say there's money but it rusted,"

Say, "Poetry's not a luxury,"
And, "I know I am space,
my body's
air," Or "This is a shape, a shape
of blood beating & cells dividing,
But outside of this shape
is space,"

Say,
"Thus the air's a luminous shadow
which accompanies
the body,"

Or,

"Poetry's the body's body,"

WATERFALL EFFECT

"As you are falling, your sense of orientation may start to play additional tricks on you, The horizon quivers in a maze of collapsing lines and you may lose any sense of above and below, of before and after, of yourself and your boundaries,"

Hito Steyerl

"Even the verse begins to eat away in the acid,"

George Oppen

I'm trying to understand this poem.
Something I wrote a decade ago.
Not just the content of it, but what
I meant by it. What it means
about me. How every word arrived
to the page as a sigh, as if *sotto voce*
had been inscribed between the lines.
How my breath, humectant, when I
read it, seemed freighted with pollen.
The air, clotted with light. For it was,
in its every fiber, an ode or reverdie:
a paean to spring. And, apropos
of that fertile season, my mother
in the poem was pregnant, seemingly
for the first time and, presumably,
with me. Or, as I put it in its first
couplet: "Something blooms
in my mother / under the covers
she is a field of wildflowers."
While I find these lines—sanguine
as they are—alarming enough

in themselves, what's stranger still
is how the poem seems to be set
vaguely in the desert. How already
my father a few couplets later
is, "A minister new frocked, /
Tending to his first flock," though
in actuality he was ordained many
years earlier and I am neither
the oldest nor only child, yet in its 8
confected pages there's nary
a whisper of my siblings, of whom
there are 6: no J or A who were born
before me, nor C who arrived
a few years after; no M or L,
who are adopted, Inuit, and sisters
by blood themselves; nor B
who, smelling like a river, came to us
much later, from an orphanage
in Addis Ababa for children who's
parents had died from AIDS.

    No.

    In lieu of this brood,
there's only inchoate little me. Me,
and my father, and mother, and
of course this covert erasure.
So what's clear from the start
is that whatever if sought
it wasn't the truth, though in its
name,

AUSCULTATION,

it certainly pretended at it—as if
listening nakedly for it. Just as
"the father," who let's admit isn't
really my father, "Presses his cool
ear there to listen, / As a chain
of daisies in her hair / On their
wedding day comes un-linked,"
and, "A gamete in the wall drifts
clean, & splits." As if he could hear
that gooey detatchment. My mitosis.
The delicate beachball of my blastula
bouncing free. But in the poem's
logic, it's this tender and domestic
fabulation—him listening to her
tummy in bed with me in it—that
for some reason reminds him
of his days spent at United Nuclear,
in the uranium mines. How he,
"Itinerate of the dark felt, a mile
deep, / In a stoner's revery,
the heat / Of the earth, molten
through a curtain / Of dirt & heavy
metals." And later, as a metaphor
of birth—my birth, I think—or
of resurrection, maybe—he recalls
rising up with the other workers,
"On elevators as big as houses /
Toward the light of sunset," where
"Bugs crackled in the haze / Like
flecks of static / As bats swooned

acrobatically / In among them,
keening / Their early evening
orrery." And I remember, as I
wrote this, imagining how, "With
only the gelid light / Of bitumen
lamps to see by, / Dawn & dusk
must have been to them / But a slim
parentheses, / Delimiting night
from day"—eliding the scene
of him breathing his breath into
the man—already dead—who'd
been thrown free of his truck—
breaking his neck—as the ambulance
flew from the mine to the hospital—
as the poem imagines instead, the relief
he must've felt to wake before dawn
on Sunday mornings, years later,
to prepare the word of the Lord,
while my mother in the poem spends
all her time sort of, "Basking in stain-
glass light," totally, "Emulsified
in a dispersion of motes, / as she
arranges lilies below his pulpit /
On oak boxes & damask," even though
she was a nurse in real life
and probably worked harder than he.

It's almost funny now, to think
think of me then with dewy, voluminous
eyes upturned and belladonna-bright,
laboring over each line and metaphor,
but what's altogether uncanny to me

now, is the sermon I composed for him
to preach; how I even went so far
as to pretend I'd transcribed it, dusting
off, "A 3M Metafine casette / Dated
5/13/1984" (Easter Sunday, I calculated:
6 months before I was born), inserting
in the midst of "his" homily lines like,
"He pauses here, I've heard it"—as if
it came straight from the archive; as if,
if asked in a court of law, I could
produce it—corroborating its existence.
But that sermon, it's as false as the idyll
itself, somehow mine, but not mine:

"Look out the window now & see
The Kingdom of Heaven in the Glory of Earth,

Spoken, ex nihilo, into being: one body,
One spirit, nothing is apart from the whole.

Consider, for instance, the bee,
Then listen to your heart

Hive-ripe, honeywise, and womblike.
Consider each cell: a hexwork abuzz

In cortex & matrix of comb.
Like the queen, you are more

Than the angel at the center
of this rind. Listen to the drone

In wattles & folds: the volt by volt
of synapses fluttering. The pallium

Of drones knows the body,
Beyond the husk, it is a lullaby

Sung by a larynx in figments.
A lexicon in movement.

The hymn and hum of a living body.
Press your ear there & feel

The throb of songs sung to outlying
Organs: every murmur, a servitude,

It cannot quit. Even, arrhythmic,
The heart seduces the body!"

I mean, Jesus. So, the bees,
they're the congregation, and the hive,
the church—I get that—but they're
also the workers, right? And the mine,
the hive? Their smell, her smell, I think—
the honeyed smell of labor and lover's
sweat; the earth and iron odor of after-
birth. But the hive is me, too, in utero,
I think: the gamete's "hexwork of cells"
etc. Or is the hive the womb, and we—
my absent brothers and sisters—we're
the bees? Anyway, I remember thinking—
and this is the height of my delusion—
that readers may see in an ampersand

in parenthesis a visual echo of the fetus
in her belly, like so: "(&—"
because the bees, aren't they also
my mother—like her, they are one
with the field of wildflowers—and
the Holy Spirit—presumably She's
the queen? But what is as yet
incomprehensible to me, is what
the ventriloquism means.

        I mean, I don't know.
Am I speaking through my father—
or is he speaking through me?
I think I thought the sermon
should be about her. About us,
together, inseparable. Nothing
to do with any dogma, only
the hidden doctrines of mother-
hood, and as I analyzed this poem
I fortuitously came upon
Donald Winnicott's "unthinkable
anxieties" of a newborn, which are
as follows:
        1. Going to pieces.
        2. Falling forever.
        3. Having no relation-
        ship to the body.
And   4. Having no orientation.

But what I find striking—and yes,
enigmatic—about this list, is how
the poem seems to be an encomium

to the pleasures of going to pieces.
Of loss of self. As it relates to new-
borns, particularly. The loss of
at least perceivable order. Or,
a tribute to maternity's profound re-
ordering. But of the many sermons
I've heard my father actually preach,
there's one fragment I remember
more vividly than any other, even
while the point—the metaphor's
tenor; the moral of the story—
as there certainly must've been one—
remains elusive to me. All that I
remember is that the central
illustration is of a comic strip
in which "our hero" trips over a
sign with the words
"BOTTOMLESS PIT"
emblazoned upon it and is sent
hurtling down through the funny
pages into the dark weeks ahead.
In my father's telling, day by day,
three panels at a time, with no
thought- or speech-bubbles trailing
away behind him, the tears that
once sped down his face run dry,
leaving tracks on his cheeks as they
grow wan then sallow, as his hair
grows long and beard fills in,
whipping away behind him, leaving
me in the pew to wonder:

    Did others follow after,

too distant to matter, too far away
to call out to— as his pants are
raveled down to rags and his
shirt, like a flag flung into the void
dissolves, revealing his ribs—

    Weren't there at least
moments of relief, brief interludes
of abandon— even as he's reduced
to a speeding skeleton—

    Mightn't some kind of
philosophy have developed,
however primitive, an ontology
of the fall—? while from the pulpit,
according to my father, his bones
were frittered away to fragments,
and the fragments, winnowed
down to dust,

Meanwhile,
in El Maspais, leaned out
on Mucinex, mixing
dexy cocktails in the
haloed pharmacy
of the car, M
rides shotgun, our
dad at the wheel,
cruising dazed
and feverish
down the highway
between Gallup
and Grants, It's
here, where the
sky is clear
under a spray
of stars, I lose
them, Where the
magnetics go
awry in the lava
fields and the
compass tilting
on the dash, as if
moved by an
invisible hand,
idles, then whirrs,
Where, as the signal

goes under in
a wash of static,
M reaches up to scan
the dial, country to
metal, turns it up
when Slipknot
comes on, then watches
her smoke flare
and loom the dome-
light, before it's whisked
out the window when
she flicks her cigarette
onto the highway
spinning away
behind her,

                    "I think she likes it,"

he says, standing
in the doorway
while I'm in bed,

                    "M, I mean, Playing
                    apothecary, Grinding
                    the pills, Mixing up
                    the syrups,"

        And it's this scene
he paints, I play back
in my head when I'm
back in New York
at my desk, staring
out from the 13th
floor at the skyline
shimmering like ice
unmelting, as if

another world
might break through
the mirage heat,
but when I turn back
to the screen, it's clear
it's no good reading
Guy Debord when
we know how fucked
we are, so I watch
instead the wind-
map in the shape
of the States C's
sent, with all its
interlocking patterns
and whorls rendered
in real-time, and
feel, if only briefly,
the breeze that rocks
the Civic where it
picks up on the other
side of the Valley
of Horses, Dad jerk
the wheel, steering
back from the rumble
strip, exhaling a
crimped Coke-can's
worth of smoke,
while in the backseat
J, M's boyfriend,
and Z, his cousin
play guitar, inventing
a kind of reservation

slowcore, trading
doped licks of Iron
Maiden, Jimi Hendrix,
Megadeth, B.B.
King, and King
Crimson,

     And it follows
me home when after
work exhausted but un-
able to sleep, I lay awake
listening to AM
call-in shows, night
preachers, conspiracy
theorists, and ufologists,
alongside bleeding-
edge therapists and
actual scientists,
discussing, station
to station, abductions,
resurrection, and
"transgenerational
hauntings," in which
sublimated psychic
material or "phantoms,"
as they would have it,
pass through the
bloodline into the
child's own sub-
conscious,

                        "A residual trauma,"

the expert says,

"works like a ventriloquist,
like a stranger within
the subject's own mental
topography,"

My dad my age on
leave from the Army,
dissipated on acid,
under the inevitable
stars, on the cliffs
of Big Sur, M's
mother, mother
of 13, pregnant
with her first
by the age M is
now, and M due
this November,
working doubles
at Sonic and
Denny's for less
than a living
wage, on the dole,
as they say, her
medical expenses
covered, as if it
were enough,
by her "Native
blood," There's
this faint dissolving
light I listen for
between the words
to help me find
sleep, No longer

visible, stretched out
to radiowaves now,
it procedes from
and permeates the
cosmos—a kind of non-
quiet, oceanic nothing—
the big bang attenuated
to static—we pick up
as Tee Vee snow,
obscuring the voices
and images I fall asleep
imagining, wake up
to the fugue of, play
back on the way to
work—a kind of familial
"Thelma and Louise"
in which we fuck up
the boys who've raped
her and suffer together
the consequences
of laws that will never
protect her,

Having accomplished
nothing, when I need a
break, I get up from
my desk, take the elevator
down and walk the 7
minutes to the park,
passing on the way
the Bon Ami
boulangerie, where,

half-catatonic in the
heat, a group of mothers
eat gelato, drink
Perrier, waiting
for their daughters
lounging down the
street on the red
carpet staircase of
the Dominican
Academy and when
I reach the park, I lay
back on on the rocks,
replace the sun with
blood, and listen for it
behind my
eyes,   A tide
that laps in the
pulse at my
neck, The artery
delicate as a shell
under my
thumb, Keeping
time, Enough to
calm my nerves,
read a poem
or two before
I put my heart
back, tuck my shirt in,
and feel above each
hip stretch-marks
like seams of
raw silk,

This body, this
cinema of the mean-
while, it's a hyper-
space of memory
and nerve I travel
through to get to
you, and when I
catch a cold I eat
too much Mucinex,
popping pills out
of the foil as I walk
to the subway
at 60th and Lex,
sweating and washing
them down with XXX
Vitamin Water
to induce a fever
that's lucid and dry
like pulling sheer
cloth across my face,
as crystals and storms
of crystals form
in my lungs
and by the time
I'm home I'm
coughing up
clots but still I eat 4
more then 4 more
till my organs
hurt and it's stupid
I know to think
consanguinity

could be achieved
through narcosis,
but it's miraculous
at least how they
clear the sinuses—
how, as if
in another
country, my
hands become out-
liers to me when I
sit down again
to write this
poem,

In the week I was back
before the bank foreclosed
on our family home,
everything was in perfect
disorder with the
symbolic precision
of a nightmare, My huge
family, the straw bale
house my father built,
mostly empty, I was
sleeping in my parents
old room, dad in L's,
M in C's, while the
rest of the beds
lay vacant, and on
the 2nd night we
stayed up late
smoking out of M's
favorite pipe, a
metal-head's novelty
shaped like a devil's
claw making the
"A-okay" gesture,
Drawing from the
wrist, schwag packed
like hot stigmata
in the palm, this sonata-
form dub-step trance
piece J composed
blaring on the laptop
ending in a montage
of every laugh

Mark Hamill ever
laughed as The Joker
in *Batman: The*
Animated Series,
and in that moment,
I found myself trying
to imagine where
I was when they
were out there, leaned
out on Mucinex,
hanging out after
a poetry reading,
probably, 2 hours
of *Cinema of the*
Present, maybe,
or at AWP, smoking
out the window of
the Harvard Ad-
vocate coat closet
when D had just
interrupted JT
in their möbius
strip dialectic on
privilege and
the place of the
other in the crisis
of infinite worlds
to survey the room
for adderall, uppers,
anything, at which
point T offers poppers
and DD sets to work

rolling a joint on a
filing cabinet, while
JT keeps repeating,

                              "There is no 'we,' There
                              is no 'we,' D, don't
                              you get it, That's the
                              thing, There is no 'we,'"

This, a brief forever
looped by virtue of
the poppers, and M

                              there is no 'we'

is rolling a joint even
slower than DD
on our kitchen table
where that spring she

                              there is no 'we'

sat filling jugs with
knock off Robitussin, Jolly
Ranchers, Mucinex, and
Oxycodone, and later, me

                              there is no 'we'

and my dad talked about
how the kids ate pills
till their kidneys hurt,
tripping in superposition,

                              there is no 'we'

shoplifting and mixing,
driving back and forth
to barter for schwag,
till the huffed drunk flange

                              there is no 'we'

of Pure Gold isobutyl

nitrites, PBR, and zinfandel,
resolve into a pre-hung
over hum and the leaden echo
goes quiet, the fluorescent
lights go out, and it's
morning and M's frying
donuts when I walk
into the kitchen, a clear
pool of lard in the skillet,
a bag of Blue Bird
flour on the counter
beside her, and even though
it's early and I haven't had
my coffee, she asks me
if I believe in demons
to which I say, "I don't know,
I guess so," but did I
mean it, thinking
of Rattray,

                    "Of poets,
               according to Jahiz,
               the best are possessed
               by genies, the next-best
               by friendly Demons,
               the average by fallen
               angels, and the bad
               by the Devil himself,"

Or was I merely moving
the conversation along,

                    "I mean think about it,"

she says,

"we all have one, Mom
has one, Dad has one
I have one, You have one,"

But it only strikes me
waiting later that week
for the plane to take me
back to Brooklyn that this
is what others mean
when they say, "soul,"
and from where I sat
on the tarmac, the
thunderheads
appeared like
guillotines
tempered in honey,
while the essence
of the air was red—
as it is each
evening at that hour
slowed—the speed
of light stopped-
gold, when nothing
seems to happen
all at once
and downpours
sublime
in the heat
above our
heads,

(TAPE FOR)
THE END OF APRIL

    Say,
I'm falling in love, Or,
that I'm falling
to pieces,

    Say the words,
"Don't go to work!"
are like an aubade always
on the tip of my
tongue,

    That today is a day
like any other, Like February,
the poem, but called
April, so not so full
of hidden pinks but all-
too-obvious champagne-
blossoming magnolias
and the sky a delft blue
bowl coming down
around us
instead,

    The coffee poured,
the grapefruit cut, the picnic
set, the big hand

stuck—say that just like
yesterday scenes like this
repeat, like the lazy
last days in a toile factory—
a surplus of cirrus like
sheer linen un-
looming above us—
while we who are forever
high in that Late
Renaissance style,
barely, if ever touch
the ground—as we tip-
toe through the tulips
on mannerist feet
and rococo cupids
compass our
heads,

 Yes, say I'm falling
to pieces, That always
in motion, still
in motion, little mortal
paranoias get
the best of me when
you're behind your
desk and I don't want to
and I don't want you
to die, Say you'll bury me
in velvet, press my
carbon into diamonds
when I do—or press
rewind before I ever

cross the threshold,
before you cross
that bridge, before you
ever leave me,
pedaling out onto
Gates like you
always do,

    I want to be
carried back through
the hours in a cloud of
fiery pale chemicals, over
the water and Vinegar
Hill, past the the steam-
spitting pipes of the
Navy Yard, the Candy
& Confectionary
Workers Local and dirt-
bath of daffodils in
the neighbor's yard,
beyond the Walt
Whitman projects
and the bordello
on Washington,
then up, fingers
finding buttons,
back to bed to
smoke between
naps and
over take-
out,

"Is Salvation
Army open on Good
Friday,"

A message
from my desk
to yours, "What better
day to pick out new out-
fits then bike to Fort
Tilden to take them
off again,"

Then you send me,
"If I Needed You,"
and I need to know, "Is it true
he used a needle to shoot
Coca Cola straight into
his arm,"

Then I send you,
"You Send Me," and go
for a walk, looking
as always for things
in the city you've never
held in your hands,
For you, I stole a grimed-
over orange railway light-
bulb right from the
socket, collected a few
fragments of subway
stalactite in front
of the man reading

HUMAN
ALL TOO
HUMAN
on the platform, "Are we
not going to do it or
are we,"

I say,

"I want to play
hooky with you
now,"

"If not, it's Easter
this weekend, let's eat acid
and bike to the Cloisters,
You could wear that black
crepe dress you bought
for holiday parties
and we can visit the room
with all the Marys
drenched in blues, holding
Christs,"

Then I send you
a little poem
called,   "Mandorla"
about the
          nebula of
          Botticelli's

          "Primavera"

how's it end—

> *fractals*
> *unfurl*

> *from within*
> *the heathen*

> *Madonna*

That's something close
to how I felt when we came
so close on New Year's
Eve eve, a spectral lace-
work endlessly repeating
out from behind
your head,

  Yes—
Say I'm falling in love,
that I'm falling to pieces,
That we sleep on the floor
on a mattress, while half
my family goes
suddenly homeless,
That the only room that's
furnished is a closet,
brimming with 100
dresses, That all the while
I've been feeling
precarious, but keeping it
private, Risking my neck,
but making it comic,

Eating my mask
and abandoning
logic, Feeling sublime,
I've been having
a gas, falling and laughing
and gasping for breath,
That all your dresses
make me jealous, That it's
because I'm in love I think
about death, Why,
shadow into heat I'll feel
kissed on the neck,
riled like a cat, even after
you're gone and all
the silks that you wear
have been worn
down to
rags,

But what I'm really
trying to say is—it's the
sum of days in the city,
lying in the High
Line's grass watching
men walk by holding
hands—all the yogis
and labour doulas of the
Upper East Side pushing
prams through Central
Park—the dozen
brides-to-be being
photographed at every

hour under weeping
willows along the
reservoirs—all
the accountants
threshing their digits
in their downtown high-
rises—the CEOs pissing
on pink urinal cakes
and the Calmic rush
of the automatic flushers
as they walk away—
it's all of us spliced
together into the beige
Mondrian, Broadway's
choked, cubicle blues—
the muzak, ersatz jazz,
the blitzkrieg klezmer
of the Xerox copier—
it's me in a box in the
sky, working, playing
DJ for Perruque Rock
Radio hour, predicting
"mortido" will be
the word of the year, dear
listener—and it's in all
of the bodies behind cash-
machines, sighing as
one as they shift
their weight from heel
to heel, humming,
"Langeweile, lange-
zeit, Langeweile, lange-

zeit," with boredom
never deep enough—it's in
knowing that it—all of
it—will end, that makes me
want to move through
the city with you as blurs
of sunlight goldly
invent a new conjunctive,
unpinning their name-
tags and unknotting
their aprons, lacking
all buttons, un-
doing all decency,
as we walk out to the
golden echo of the exit
bells' chime, where
together for now amid
the panoply of glass
and applewax asterisks
solarizing every surface
we'll be torn limn-
from-limn as the f-
stop of the avenue
opens past
aperture—

That following summer
I left the city for a friend's farm
just south of Albuquerque
and after dinners,
in the evenings' cool,
we'd go out to collect
the eggs, sharing
a cigarette between us
and sipping dark rum
from small porcelain
cups, The Korean erotica
embossed on the side
more a fact than a sign,
the clavicle, knee, dipped
neck, the shoulder
slipping its shirt,
recalling a boy I'd seen
at a poetry reading
before I'd left,
I'd thought of often
after, His flannel slung
low, head tilted, the
strap of his tank-top
exposed, At the end
of our rounds, in the far
field, one particularly large
black hen had taken

up roost in the disused
drawers of an apiary
that now housed
a copper spigot and
when I'd open the lid
she'd evacuate
like a ghost, heart-
stopping, into
the gloaming,
leaving her eggs
in their nest of
weeds, planetesimal,
eclipsed, and still
warm to the touch,
The grey hexes' waxen
remnants of a hive
still clung in the corners,
and sweaty and cool
the tap fed a small ring
of fruit trees nearby,
where, early in the
season, sudden shoots
of asparagus, fresher
and sweeter than any
I'd had or have had
since, stood miraculously
tall in the grove,
Finishing our cigarette,
we'd pick and eat one
each on the way
back to the house
as the light blending

in with the day-
moon going down
made a capsizing
kind of motion over
the fields, Sugar
in the blood, A
compulsive cinema
of repetitious labor
replaying—as if as a habit
of the eye—the task
which only hours earlier
had ceased, Night after
night lost to insomnia,
The bright, almost day-
glo scape I'd snipped by day
flickering caution-yellow
in the corneas' neon
garden by night,
Having lost the house,
weekend visits
home only added to this
restless state, going back
and forth between
my folks as they waited
for the divorce to settle,
Taking M out for donuts
and coffee if she could
be found, I took all this
as a challenge to exhaust
myself, Rode for
miles in that lagging
dusk light, the ancient

acequias which for
centuries had irrigated
the farmlands flashing
in the darkening fields
like stripes of light on
gun-metal leading
down to the Rio
Grande,

It was as if by habit
then, that when I returned
to the city in June, for
a week, for a job, the first
thing I did was molly and ride
along the Hudson and on
through the FiDi at night,
imagining the high-
rises full of slumbering
bankers, the statistics,
dreaming, I'd been told
many times money
has no memory, is liquid,
fungible, but in the vacant
corridors of Wall St.
I could sense the algorithms
like great spirits writhing
in the dark, I'd done
a fair amount of
reading up on the drug
before taking it, and while
some claim ecstasy is
inconvenient—a dopamine

suck—others say it's
anathema to PTSD,
and though I've
only got your average
workaday anxieties to
break, little hungers
glimpsed there in the eyes'
saccade, I couldn't
help imagining handing
M the pills and watching
her trauma crumble
away,

    I remember I kept
hoping he'd reach out
to me when sick on
stolen champagne
I told all of this to the
boy from the poetry
reading months later,
but it was as if another
country rose up between
us as I spoke and before
I'd finished he turned
his face from mine to
puke among the rocks
where the water laps
along the banks
of the East River,
This was years ago
now and I think he
moved out West some-

where where the land-
scape degrades at such
a rate the maps will still
be good in 10,000 yrs
or more, As for M, she
took up meth 8 months
ago but kicked it again
like 6 months later, on
her own, so she could
see her girls again,
There are 4 or them
now, was almost a 5th,
and for the time-being
they're living with her
best friend's ex—an ex-
military cop with a big
heart, 3 huge dogs,
and a gun safe just in-
side the door of his
small ranch-style home,
Last month I was there
and watched them line
up one by one in their
living room to have her
paint their nails in
purple sparkles, Hands
gentle, shaking a little,
And just now, tonight, he
sent a half-dozen photo-
graphs of them posing
under junipers in hand-
sewn, particolored dresses,

which makes me feel,
I don't know where I am,
what story I'm telling any-
more, always half-
looking back—the phantom
current of a dying river 2,000
miles away, still stronger,
more real than the current
of any river however
near I've never touched—
the sky grey, blue, rust
pink, when finally we'd reach
the Bosque's cool, we'd
leave our bikes in the dust,
walk out under the heavy
rotting cottonwoods, to wade
naked, ankle-deep, knee-
deep into the slurry while
above us, from the river's
wide plain, the wildfire's
haze hung in the sky and
the moon in the east, smoked
red, strabismic, set
with the sun,

When I was 6 or so
Rush Limbaugh was always
on the radio, and I was
always in the family
station wagon
running errands
with my dad,
Mondays, he liked
to buy a dozen
day-olds at the
Puritan Bakery
down the street,
to eat them while
he wrote his sermons,
and drank his coffee
black, While I
waited in the car,
I couldn't help it,
I was drawn to that
voice, its rhythm
coming through
the speakers, that
disembodied rasp,
I remember he'd
read a litany of men
who'd died, press
a button, and wait

for the canned applause
to quiet, and though
the terms were big
the gist was clear
so over the years
I pieced it all together
from the way
people laughed when
me and my best friend
called each other
"husband," from how
the older boys talked
and, in the fields
one summer, from P's
need to secretly
touch me, and I remember
learning, I forget
when, the disease
could live in your blood
for years, For years
I thought one day
I'd get sick or
suddenly die,
It could have been
that week, that
month, or that same
evening, after listening
to Rush on the radio,
a rattler came gliding
out of the high dry
grass where I was
playing, But just like that

my dad, when I went
to get him, with a spade,
five jabs, and a flick, cut
the head from the body,
leaving it in five even
pieces in the dust—
and I remember over
supper how he told us
how the poison works,
How it turns the skin
black and kills
the cells so wounds
won't close, How the
little ones are
worse, not yet knowing
how to staunch
the venom's flow,
I finished my meal,
I cleared my plate,
I went outside,
The sun was going down,
and in the yard
I sat in the dust
watching the dizzy-
patterned lengths
sluggishly still
writhing, rasping
free of the spade's
shallow pan, leaving
ornate loops of black
blood in the pale
red sand, I could

see where the poison
pooled, occluded,
like vinegar in the tips
of its fangs, as the slits
of its eyes stared
at nothing and its mouth
opened and closed
upon nothing—as if it
were trying to tell
a secret, yet nothing
coiled there to
speak it,

RESURRECTION ROCK

it's true we called them pigs

said we hated them
feared them

said fuck them
when they weren't around

I guess that was the animus

why without thinking
we ducked the CAUTION ribbon
hanging over the arroyo
where it interrupts the path

the air
the space around it
the slow censer of the sun
a scent of sage wafting over us
and that ribbon quietly fluttering
holding it all in place

if I'm honest
without it
we never would noticed
the bones half-
buried further up

the bight

the raw burl
of the arm's
unsocketed ball
for instance
jutting
from the cut

or further downstream
a half-dozen vertebrae
like scrying dice
scattered loose of the spine
in the dried-up
rivulet

as if the earth
had coughed them up

out there in the air with the light shining on them
they seemed to rearrange the landscape
around them
all those easter sunrise services
when we were kids
we'd never seen them
all those times as teens
as was the case that evening
we'd gone there to smoke
and watch the sun set
over the hogbacks
to lay back
and wait for the stars

to start falling
they were there
waiting
100 yards or so
the "wrong side"
of the graveyard fence
for the flash flood
to exhume them or the wind
to sift them free

so of course I was surprised
to find myself there
kneeling over the skull
its orbitals like an hourglass
the lower half
half-filled with sand
and as we ducked back under
the ribbon and continued
on our way I kept thinking
of the sockeyes'
return

how they read the odor
of the river like a map
the taste of the till
washing into it
like a tether
leading them
back

how leaning over the bridge
in early fall

where the current turns turbid
as it enters the ocean
my grandfather told me
they'd given up eating already
exchanging
our more ordinary hungers
for another

that even then as their deep red forms
coursed against the current
the current was pulling them apart
a confetti of scales
sluiced from skin as their muscles burned
every last calorie until
as if unlocked
by that elusive bouquet
of home
they'd relinquish
their lode to the river
and with it
their bodies
as well

and yet it wasn't the ones who made it
I found myself lingering over
but those fish who
like this stranger
seemed to have fallen short
of their final destination
unmarked
discarnate
the very fact of their nakedness

hanging unanswered
like a question
in the air

had they been a sinner
unworthy
forsaken interloper
or did they come to rest here
long before God
ever claimed this plot
as another of His acres

he came here as a missionary
after the war
my father's father
that old pilgrim
I still picture him
polishing his rifle
in the afterlife
these lands no more
stolen than any other
in this country
and still feel acutely nothing
I can say can undo
the good deeds
he'd thought he'd done
though they are to me nothing more
than another step
in the slow destruction
of a people he knew
and loved
and as the evening wore on

and we lay back on the rock
and watched the meteors fall
and dissolve in the dark
paying out their forms
for brief moments of light
I wandered down into
the graveyard
picking my way
by the aqueous glow
of solar powered l e d's
while the light
and a slight pentacostal noise
carried across the field
from a revival tent
on the edge of 66

the air cool
still on my skin
as I watched an occasional car
move into the darkness
I found myself
thinking of that painting
by Paul Klee
the one with the clock
clicking away
at its dark heart
its cartoon arithmetic
the fish and its sulfurous figures
because like the sockeye
I've always wanted to know
what it is about that inner-governor
secreted away inside them

those first subterranean fish who
even as the cave commits
its brute depth
swim on
nonetheless
abandoning light
for blindness

scototropic or
troglomorphic
is what they call it

shrugging
their color down
the bloodline
their cold roe
like pale ellipsis
swirling
in the mineral dark
as their offspring turn
almost to silk
in jaw
and gill
until
one day their eyes
seal over
becoming more
current
now
than fish
only living in a sense
by vibration

and alchemical
tongues—
a pause
on the way
to nothing—
a draft
in the gene-
pool a-
drift

and as I made my way
through the dark
back to the rock
maybe I should have guessed
but I'd been too poor
to go home for the funeral
so I knew but didn't know
that of course
he was buried here
when I found his name on a stone

RICHARD KRUIS
1917 - 2008

the way it stood there
grey in its plainness
too ordinary
its vacancy filled me
and as my spine conformed
to the contour of the rock
I felt a hollow kind of closure
at the thought of those other bones there

as if washed clean
like an empty vessel with its stopper in it
the liquid marrow
bottled and warm
at how quiet he was
and how
with a kind of singing
in the fissures
that hold me together
for the moment
I wasn't

KALPA

A lunar smudge
on the horizon's edge; an angel
in rags, traipsing the void.
The stars—dispersed—
like the crystal ramparts
she's brushed down to dust
with the hem of her once-
silken robes, the mountain-
top floating up beneath me
erodes at the rate it rises
& the river that winds
like a brass wire below
divides the massif in two.
From this side of the divide
I want to speak, not in pure
language, but of pure duration.
To ask, "What's katabasis
& where'll your honey-
moon be if the sky's an oasis
no longer, but an inferno?
If you're still out there, waiting
like La Llorona or Hagar,
even—with mouth up-
turned, aphasic with thirst—
in the shadow of a cloud
that can't make its rains
reach the river-

bed they evaporate
above,"

WATERFALL EFFECT

$2,15/hr + tips
and elsewhere dark money
changes hands,

Look away
and the bottles and plates,
salt and pepper,
coffee cups, half 'n' half
and sugar, everything
levitates,

you & me
you & me
you & me
you & me
you & me
you & me
you & me
you & me
you & me
you & me

printed in red and green
on the server's T-
shirt,

In the photo of the diner

on the diner's wall, imagine how
the model's pearls, from the
viewfinder inverted,
would've clattered,
seemingly
spilling
into the air,

    Having a Coke,
Her cashmere cardigan, gingham
skirt, The red clock
ticking back-
wards
below her head,

    "Mise-en-abyme,"
That's the term,
Hot oil, burnt
sugar, "All my diamonds
shine cause they're really
diamonds," playing
on the radio,

    I hold her baby, We smoke
her cigarettes, She asks me
if I like to party,

    big-Business.
& little bumps of yay
behind the grease trap, Thus
hidden
from CCTV,

A new science
for every object, For every object
a new song,
and like little knots of flame
going cold, all my diamonds
are slowly turning
back to coal,

GOLD LEAF

in inviolate
violet hours
w/ the sun
rising or coming
down like wine
w/ diamonds
in the glass
lavender
in that way
& benthic
almost
at the center
when the work
day has ended
or is yet to begin
& I can't sleep
so I think
of sleep
listening at
dawn for
the canned
muezzin from
the mosque
on Fulton
while the gulls
outside
my window

floss the thermals
in recursive arcs
then waiting
for the answer
an hour later
from the midi
carillon tolling
"this world
is not my
home," on
simulacral bells
an ersatz aubade
I listened to
w/ C, violet
in inviolate hours
the air the same
bright tense
manic present
perfect in
purpureal sheets
our nerves
blended beyond
the boundary
of the body
watching her descent
into the subway
gemini orbital
in mercurial boots
on the darkside
of the avenue
like a workaday
orphic Brel

not exactly discreet
from the wind
the gulls' shadowy
arcs eclipsed
by deeper shadows
how did the dancers
who survived her
describe their love
having moved so long
in ways she'd moved
they knew themselves
as part of her
hic jacet Pina in tics
in gestures as if
translating
through dance
one phrase
from Rimbaud
in perpetuum
inviolate violet
in hours interred
in nerve & twitch
having come up
as the sun went
down w/
B & E, what we
hoped for
was a kind of code
cracking utterance
or syntagm's
abruption like "I
is another

too" w/ candles
lit & all around
drinking tea
having listened
to Palestrina
or Josquin's
"Mille regretz"
melismatic & erasing
spit loud
in the choral throat
I think we came close
w/ the light
sustained
like a final note
before resolve
ex cathedra
& cold filled
w/ gulls
gliding the contra
alto lacing
the baritone
up & weaving
through the kyrie
as if ascending
via portapro
the Brooklyn Bridge
w/ the skyline
ablur like a gob
of Tee Vee snow
stars twinkling
in the aspic
but it's all sanskrit

& rainbows cast
on gilded rafters'
gold leaf to me
sitting up here
near the chandeliers
of exploded
Swarovski motif
holding a pair
of nosebleed
tickets to the MET
me & N occupying
opera seats
if only for a night
pink pinstripes
smoldering
like contrails
in the low velvet dark
as we watch far below
a fattened primo
uomo arpeggiate
the early life
of Gandhi
lost in the Koch
& Glass fungible
bel canto
while downtown
the pigs tune up
their sirens
& head for the Park
I want to say
we were dreaming
when the cuffs went on

of the spandrel
magenta in the
interstice
of lights
flashing *red*
blue *red* blue
red blue
caring very little
for plot but texture
longing for more from
art's objects than mere
displays of wealth
& were reduced
ourselves
to mere objects
amid objects
w/o a center
under the duress
of impossible
love always loving
what is yet
to come or has
since
disappeared,

or as B put it
in the Holiday
Inn Express
in Cincinnati
the night before
we met D
for drinks

at the Comet,
ironically
but w/ total
sincerity
"Arbitrary
demarcation,
dude," the
dancers the
dancer
the dance
like how D
eyes lifted
to the ceiling
sometimes
sometimes w/
an explanatory
gesture of his hand
rising as if
of itself w/
a lilt or
murmur
spoke of music
& his friend G
as if each were
throughout
our lives
the way nerves
are throughout
our bodies
inviolate
in violet hours
their names' private

memories illicit
luxuries always
on the tips
of our
tongues,

REGRESSION

"Cold winds blowing
And life looks like some malignant disease,
Viewed from the heights of reason
Which I don't believe in,"

Bernadette Mayer

"You murmur your magic (what help is the past?):"

Lorine Niedecker

LIKE LIFE

After Visiting "Like Life: Sculpture, Color,
& the Body (1300 - Now)"

On the other side of the curtains
that divide up the rooms, indistinct,
if only briefly, the silhouettes
of statues & patrons seem to blend—
as if both were made of marble,
as I must've seemed to them.
Like the painting of the saint
praying to a statue of a saint:
reverential, silent, they face
one another, and the material
so slight between us, a breath
or the barest gesture, disturbs
the air. They seem almost stalled
here, never having known death,
yet lingering too close to life—
as if there were a sympathetic
magic in the materials used.
A slight blush, an animating
glamour in the slush wax flesh
of the anonymous, anatomical
venus; in the gold-leaf & velvet
queen. A song as much in Salome's
demoniac eyes of shell & amber,

as in the écorché of the day-
laborer's life-size red frame
of papier-mâché & painted plaster.
And how often through wealth
& ease, & how often through need—
or whatever was ready-to-hand—
seemed legible not in craft or lack
thereof, but in this more elemental
grammar. I must have been still
under that same spell as I paid
for *The Autobiography of Alice
B. Toklas* at the outdoor bookstore
on the corner of the park after close.
I must've needed to see your face,
because there you were, two years
gone this September, standing a
few tables off, in the figure
of a stranger,

REGRESSION

fall

for Carolyn (1990-2016)

"Relinquishment,"

At least that's what they say,
When the haggling's done, the act of opening
the hand, But if it ever truly ends,
in between are phases the experts
will never recognize, Interleaved with disbelief
and fury, delirium, glossolalia,
hysterical nostalgia, etc.
Or the stage in which one eats too much
Xanax, gummy bears, and caviar
from the bodega around the corner, "takes a nap"
facedown, listening to the neighbor's
old soul records
filtered through the floorboards,

As for me, I keep attempting
rational sentiments despite myself, Cold comfort,
an architecture of tics in rhetoric,
Like, "It's no good hoping for accuracy
from the flowcharts that mark grief's progression,"
"The swamp after all is not the map,"

And, "And yet, one longs for an argument
nonetheless, The 'In which'
in which the plot is laid bare,
as in *Paradise Lost* or other
arcane texts,"

     What comes next,

          Savoring almost nothing
before grief resurges, what remains is the tension
of the chiastic structure
and its spillage, As if it were an accident,
when describing the origins of good and evil,
that a hero was made of the fallen one,
How "elegiac" rolls off the tongue
with an unacknowledged hush at the beauty
of others' sorrow, The Devil in the details,
or the accumulation of velleities
so many I know and love
would ascribe to God's catastrophic hand,

          Over coffee in L.A.,
having dreamed away the night beside each other
as chaste as brother and sister,
you said you felt the opposite when I tried to recall
the taxonomy of mediocre poets
possessed by evil spirits, How the Devil guides
the worst poets' pens, Angels,
the best, etc., But I never had the chance to ask you
what you thought the difference was,
Like me, you were appalled by angels
you didn't believe in, yet still knew what it meant

to be brushed by the weight of their hem
and baffled, A campy kind of aporia,
like, "Every angel is terrifying,
well-built, and adorned in flame
and lamé,"

Still cross-eyed with desire,
Still longing to see what the future holds,
How can I employ reason
to make myself feel what I know to be true
when you're the one who animates
my disbelief, lingering like the day that's over
but clings to your nerves a while,
"Still wading sentimentally in a year,
That ended sentimentally in the middle of a season,"
is how you put it, Like lying still
on a summer's evening with the impress of
the pool's blue sway rippling through
your equilibrium,

An intaglio of motion,
It washes over you,

And you wake with a start,
Lift your face from the floorboards to return
to the freezer to freshen your drink,

And you read,
as if by instinctual misprision,
"You surround me,"
to mean a kind of dysphoria, As in,
"Who is this body I'm embedded in,"

It leaves you breathless,
"Who are these people,"
That old refrain, "This can't be life,"
How it must feel to find your own words
in quotes, "The body's body,"
As if, if you're anything,
you're "the flattening of so many
into one being," Possessed,
not relinquished, Drowning in,
or swaddled by them,
A channel through which grief returns
refreshed, the way the river traces
the bed it carves, on the surface
unchanged, yet deepened,

    "You surround me,"

Is this what true love feels like,

This bitter Earth,
and nonetheless yearning out of season
for saturnalian rites of over-
saturation,

A bloodbath and nonetheless the sky
and dusky hydrangeas' sopping blues
and purples, terminally
in bloom,

When the automatic knell
irrupts the disco's vesper in this new dark age,
I hear it like an open invitation
to declare my love for sentimentality,
Afterall, don't they say, "Reason is,"
in a certain light,
"The mere sentiment of those who can afford
to believe in a rational world,"
But what, I want to know,
cuts without hesitation to the quick,
If you say, "Say her name,"
say it again,

In opal light, for instance, In liquid
crystal display light, The flimmer

of vaporizer light, or the phone screen relucent
across the cab's backseat
idling in the hospital's
shadow, In the strobe of red
and blue light-
emitting-diodes, In the night-
club's magenta pulse,
In the idiorrhythmic trace of the heart
rate monitor, Belying
delirium,

       Drift,

spring

Q,

    What's the saddest music in the world,

A,

    It's either me singing, "Sign 'O' the Times"
cover to cover or all of the times
someone like you has wondered, "But how much survives,
How much of any one of us
survives," Seemingly granting us all permission
to hate ourselves
less,

    3:22 of a Thursday,
arriving at the pearly gates via perverse kinesis,
Prince has died,
and I remember when the playlist labeled "paradise"
was empty, As if, if only briefly,
everything ceased being everything,
yet the record's dark arrondissement went on spinning
anyway, even after the needle
had lifted,

    Imagine murmuring,
"Goodbye, cruel world,"
then leaving behind a vault
of silently blistering
solos, "Goodbye,"

and a selfie in a 16th C, vanity,
Or a saint's flayed
skin,

    Alone, reading "Dirty Poem,"
it's clear the body has enough
to reckon with within itself, "sugars [foaming]
in the pulp," The invisible apothecary,
"brewing its own alcohols," etc.

    But the doctor's explanation is simple,
if enigmatic, The silver palomino,
pent up and anxious, dances as if on stilettos,
nipping at her flanks
till she bleeds,
As if "hacking" her own nervous system,
she floods her enormous body
with wine,

winter

    It seems slow at this distance
and calmly fatal, A slight nova, Insignificant
diamonds and rings of irrelevant
silk, On the phone's screen, twin blue suns turning
a deeper blue, Torqued
and twisting deeper as they slow, each collapsing
into the vortex of the other,
These far-distant blackstars, under this filter,
are not unlike the fluorescent cells
in the cervix and ovaries, highlighted by dyes,
marking our mothers' cancers'
growth, Out of reach, Light swallowing light,
and briefly,
an eclipse-green autophagy,

    Or like the ultrasound
grayscale twins growing where their sister
grew before them
in my sister's womb, The tissues,
like heatwaves, flowing off
of bright white
masses,

    But what does it mean
if all the colors are false,
The space-age purr of the heavenly bodies,
mere artifice,

As the end advances,
will the seasons accelerate in their rhythms,

Spring,
and then spring again,

You can't simply re-apply the emulsion
crumbling from the tapes,
then listen,

Listen again,

fall

  The calendars are wrong,
The weather's wrong too, 72°
early in the evening
in early November, warm enough out
to read "Neon Clouds"
in a cheap silk shirt, starry-night-like
and overlaid with pinwheels,
Go down, sip Arak
on the stoop,

  A splash of cold water,
An instant pearl,

  I remember leaving
Tibor de Nagy on a night like this,
puking vertiginously
at 56th and Park, thinking
of Lisa Robertson saying
something like, "Psychology oozes
from every object,"

  Something rattles
in my skull, A lily-of-the-valley
in my jaw, Little more
than florilegia and a deathdrive,
Still I want to know,
who of you will invent a new metric,

that which can be measured
in erratic tonnage,
in moraines
exposed,
etc.

    Murmuring, "Goodbye,
green world," As "Another Green World"
enters and exits
our orbit, At 180 grams
it decays as it spins,
and we only ever listen at the height
of summer, which seems just
to have passed, but is,
no doubt,
quickly approaching,

summer

    Intergalactic
weather patterns,
Interstellar
winds,
etc.

    A bloom of mould
on a spear of wheat, Spoors,
sifting the dark, Virgo,
Gemini, Pisces, It's
summer, It's
spring,
It's winter,
and the zodiac twists
in the brassy muzz
where music
bleeds together
above
the rooftops,

    Where, when I follow
the glowing path
of the searchlight over
the city, I try but fail to feel
only for whatever's
outside my window,
or trapped

between the glass,

A few roaches,

A glacial nosegay
of blue-bottle husks
and cigarette
butts,

The warped
circle of moons, refracted,
Enmillioned
somewhere else on the tides,

spring

    The PH levels
in the soil are on my mind, AC units
on warmish spring days
dripping dew
down onto kudzu, Black acorns
the wind's combed out,
rotting,

    It's nasty dirt to grow anything in,
but with plenty of acid
the hydrangeas are a creamy sapphire
in that corner & a basic purple
where there's none,

    Their corymbs drift without fixity,

    Every time I look up
names for clouds I find a new one,
The latest, "nacreous,"
means "mother-of-pearl" "pigeon-
neck purple"
or "gill-of-trout,"

    Was it only yesterday
I watched our new neighbors
replace the cupid
in the garden with a skull,

spring

It's Easter this weekend
and today it seems that even these bodies
we carry with us hang around us
like a burden of flowers, These emblems
that provoke us to speak
in the pastel codes of grief,
Of how the bloom is off of the red rose
and the carnation, Of narcissus'
infinite recursive consumption,
and asphodels' elysian fields,
Of the bruises like forget-me-nots
stippling a loved-one's skin,
and of Io's craters' quiet crocus—
the clabber of topographic salts
on the sheets, This ecology
of hidden engines that drive us
through the mornings, in the times
between, to sweeten the reed
with spit, the acrid clef, to sing
the song of the anemone, the anemic,
the melancholic at the window,
To contemplate the everblooming
amaranth of N's womb,
in which a cyst the size of a dahlia
quietly grows,

Sugar in my eyes
when the sun goes
down, Everything slowly turning
a misty blue as the shadows shift—
tenebris in lux to lux
in tenebris, Shuffle
of foam over the rocks
on the bank and the music-
box on the water-
front canters lacquer
horses up and
down through the milk-
of-marigold sodium
lamp light,

Unnding on the bridge,
New Year's Unir champagne
cages in my pockets, I'm I drunk
on my own blood again,
A shuffle of foam over the ears
and the background
fades away,

A spliff of sage and hash,
listening to "Mille Regretz,"
with the cupids crushed,
and the lenses cracked

& love or w/e we have
on hand
like vaseline
sealing
the fissures,

fall

     When Lou Reed died
Laurie Anderson wrote, "I believe
the purpose of death is the release
of love," And it's true,
We filled thermoses with sangria,
got wasted in the park,
Spent the day flipping *Berlin*
A to B, B to A,
Clicked repeat and looped
"Sunday Morning"
all afternoon, Repeat,
and cried in public,

     In his last interview,
the drawstrings
of his scrubs drawn tight,
it's clear he's dying,
But he says,

       "There's a sound you hear in your head,

       It's your nerves or your blood running,

       It's kind of amazing to hear that,

       You're in a hospital,

You have an ultrasound and they turn it up,

You hear your blood flowing,"

    He claims to sleep
with his guitar, Claims he never practiced,
never was taught, but "played
from the heart," and as he fades
to black he murmurs,
    "My life is music,"
As if that's all it was, blood-noise
feeding back to blood,
that closed-circuit's vital infinity,
a living fugue
too quiet to hear,
As if, amplifying his body's
last days' drone
might preserve him, turn him
revenant under
the needle, Even with the instrument
destroyed,
we keep the song,

summer

    Awake before I mean to be,
Feeling religious when I don't want to be,
Surveying the ephemera
of my life,

    The xeroxed poems
and books I have but haven't read,
The few scraps of handwritten
"Mornings" torn out
to stuff my pockets with, memorize,
and toss out,

    The notebooks filled
with Xs struck through lengthy strophes
on tics and nervy twitching,
as if I could redact the surge of yen,
compose an ode instead
to the pathetic fallacy
which defines
my life, To the bluster
of irrational winds, The bludgeoning
brutish light of summer,
To winters lived for magenta,
twilit eyelids, and keyhole tans
when you blink,

    And to spring,

To April and the promise
of lines as endless and recursive as scenes on toile,
sublingual, yanked in a smooth stream
from the throat, as if spooled
where the heart belongs,

To bright bolts
inscribed with cupid shrines
and fountainheads with frothing arcs
of never-falling water, Ruffling
the air, Waiting,
yes,

A helical furl
of electrical woad, A funerary shroud
with arabesques
you can bury me in,

But in the meantime,
another season wants to come
and change the contents
of my blood
again,

I can feel it,
Is there a better way to put it,

No,

The body's body's air's ore's not a luxury—
it's a luminous shadow,

Always there,

　　For what but the tips
of the fingers, the tip of the tongue,
is the locus of luxury,
What but the eye
is the house of taste, filigreed
with phonemes, Like the dark oak
outside my window, its inner-
creaking and the leaves
that hush it,
when new light fills it, it moves
the way a river does,
mimicking itself, Dark leaves
and leaf-cut light,
each time new, yet somehow
always the same,

　　How the words dissipate
as soon as they leave
your lips, Slow
time,
but cannot reverse it,

ACKNOWLEDGMENTS

These poems do too little to acknowledge the persistent and historical damage done to the tribes who are the rightful stewards of the territories in which they were written. These include the lands of the Dine, Zuni, Pueblo, Lenape, Wappinger, Canarsie, Matinecock, and Nauset tribes. Over 70 years ago my family arrived in Dine territory as missionaries and I am particularly troubled by their part in the erasure of the cultures, languages, and communities of The People who live there. I know too well the insufficiency of good intentions; this acknowledgement does nothing to remediate my family's part in this colonial project. Rather, it is just that: an acknowledgment and a lamentation.

To Benny, Tyler, Natalie, and Dan, with special love and thanks to Eli— my inadvertent patron— and to my dear friend Patty Gone. To my family at Wendy's Subway, past, present, and future. To Matt Longabucco, my closest and kindest reader, and to Rachel for being a bulwark and a visionary. To Judah Rubin, Erin Morrill, MacGregor Card, Caroline Gormley, David Hutcheson, Corinne Schneider, Sara Martin, Laura Neal, Austin Segrest, Philip Matthews, Wilder Alison, Adjua Gargi Nzinga Greaves, Jenny Zhang, Stacy Szymaszek, L.S. Klatt, Kevin Killian, Dottie Lasky, and Dana Ward— and to all of the poets who've helped me continue to see the viability and vitality of poetry in the world. To Tom, Cody, Kyle, Casey, Jono, and Paula. Most of these poems were begun at the Hunter College MFA and completed at the Fine Arts Work Center in Provincetown; special thanks to my peers in those places and to Donna Masini, my collaborator Jan Heller Levi, and Tom Sleigh, who has been my greatest supporter, mentor, and critic; to Josh Weiner and Major Jackson for your encouragement; and to Rebecca Connor and Eve Levy, who helped me make my way. Thank you Vert and Lydia for taking me in.

To friend to poets Nicole Eisenman, for the use of her painting, *Golden Showers*.

Chris and Nick, you've been incredibly generous editors, thank you for working to make this come true.

Finally, to mom, dad, J, A, C, M, L, & B: I love you all.

Thanks to the editors of the following publications for seeing value in my work:

"Auscultation" in *A Perfect Vacuum*; "Mucinex" in *Atlas Review*; "April" with *Well Greased Press*, as well as "Bosky farm," which was reincarnated in *Frontier Poetry*; "The Rattler" in *Quadrant*; "Resurrection Rock" at the *Pen Poetry Series*; "Waterfall effect" at *Cosmonauts Avenue*; "Gold Leaf" in *Elderly*; "Like Life" in *Southword*; "Regression" in *The Brooklyn Rail*.